# Recruitment Hacks

# By

# Joseph Henry

☐

☐

# Introduction

The Naked Recruiter is proud to bring you the Life Hacks that will improve the running of your desk, your business, help you smash your sales targets and become the best recruiter you can be.

All whilst getting a great night's sleep. We all know recruitment is one of the hardest, most challenging, mentally demanding careers out there. Many people do not make the grade. However, if you use our Life Hacks then you will become less stressed, more productive and more successful.

# Why have we created Life Hacks for Recruiters?

Recruiters need help to make their lives easier and more fulfilling daily.

Much of the way that recruitment works is stuck in the dark ages of 1980's and 1990's telephone sales business model. The telephone is always going to be king in recruitment, but why do we still do so many blind cold calls? Why are so many recruitment companies so digitally naïve and why does recruitment not seem to be changing?

Essentially these questions kicked off the entire Naked Recruiter website and we are now trying to bring new thinking into recruitment via thenakedrecruiter.com and our Life Hacks series as outlined in this wonderful book

# So who Am I?

My name is Joseph Henry or Henry to my friends or much worse to my enemies. Don't worry I do not have enemies as I am lovely really. I just said that to make an impact.

My recruitment career started a decade ago after a brief stint working in insurance and then politics. Since then I have worked for a big multinational executive search firm, a well know high street agency, a political services provider who also had a recruitment agency that I turned around, and now run my own business.

As a hobby and creative outlet, I also write a popular blog called the Naked Recruiter – just google "the naked recruiter".

# What is a Life Hack?

*"Life hack (or life hacking) refers to any trick, shortcut, skill, or novelty method that increases productivity and efficiency, in all walks of life. The term was primarily used by computer experts who suffer from information overload or those with a playful curiosity in the ways they can accelerate their workflow in ways other than programming."*

For this book I wanted to bring the spirit of the life hack into recruitment. Not to talk that much about cold calls, all recruitment books seem to talk about cold calls, but a whole myriad of ways that we as a recruitment community can get better, more productive and just a little bit sassier.

I hope you enjoy the book. If you have any questions, please email me at joseph@thenakedrecruiter.com

# Prepare tomorrow the night before

It is the end of the long and tiresome day. You just want to get out of the door, get home and open a cold one from the fridge. The temptation to just leave the office is great, almost unbearable and writing that to-do list feels like such a chore.

STOP RIGHT THERE!

Every evening you should prepare your next day before leaving the office. This should be part of your end of play ritual. Even 10 minutes planning can save you hours the next day and make sure that you are able to get started first thing before procrastination kicks in.

The real benefits of creating a to-do list every day are:

Clears your head at the end of the day of all the little things that you need to do that you might forget by tomorrow.

Gives you your first task to-do the next day meaning you have fewer decisions to make and get the ball rolling early.
Focuses your work on a proactive mindset rather than a reactive state as you come into the office first thing.

Anthony Robbins the famed chisel-jawed self-help guru and author of Awaken the Giant Within said *"Losers React, Leaders Anticipate"* wise words.

If you are struggling to come up with a format for your to-do list why not try
https://monday.com/

# Tidy your desk each

# evening

\*\*\* Sounding like your mother Klaxon\*\*\*

Yes, in this post I am going to sound a little bit like your mother, telling you to tidy your room. However, tidying your desk will have a very positive impact on your working life. So please stay with me.

Having a tidy desk will make you more productive and will reduce your stress levels at the end of the day and the start of the next one.

Why is tidying your desk a key element in productivity and stress reduction? In part, it comes down to three core elements:

Ritual Ending to the day: It creates an end of the day ritual, which when combined with some of our other Life Hacks will signal the end of stressful workday and begin a period of rest.

Declutters your desk and mind: Reduces the friction when you arrive at your desk in the morning by removing everything that is not vital and putting it into the bin or into the right desk draw.
It leaves your workspace clean and increases mental focus in the morning on your to do list, and not clutter.

Gives a sense of pride: Your desk is the location you make real change happen in people's lives, so having it look clean and professional will also help you feel clean, well organised and professional. With the added bonus that it will make you look professional and in control to your colleagues and managers.

# Turn off your PC last thing

# at night

At the end of working day there is no nicer feeling than clicking the shutdown button and seeing the computer start to turn off. It is a lovely way to end the day nicely and is also good for your productivity.

So why is turning you PC or Laptop of at night good for your productivity?

Firstly, shutting down your PC and automatically updating will keep the software up-to date which should, hopefully, keep you busy and productive as updates should keep the software ticking over and ironing out any bugs.

Secondly, turning off your PC or Laptop has a lovely mental effect that it signals to you that the working day has now ended and now is the time for rest and relaxation.

Thirdly, in the morning as you turn on your PC and let it load up it will give you time to review your to-do list and get that coffee you will need to kick ass throughout the day.

# Write a To Do List

It has been a long and very hard day. You have been a maestro on the phones. Candidate calls. Client Calls. Dealing with a no-show candidate and getting that deal in (you dancer!) and now it is the end of the day.

The temptation to go to the pub, or head home and get a cold one from the fridge or pour out a nice glass of red is very high indeed.

**STOP RIGHT THERE!**

Leaving now without doing a to-do list will leave you rudderless and slow to get going. Write a to do list and keep the momentum going tomorrow.

If I come across as a little preachy that is because I am being preachy.

To Do Lists are one of the biggest hallmarks of success. From Benjamin Franklin to Stephen Covey to Elon "I send cars into space" Musk all swear by to do lists.

Some people when beginning with the to-do list revolution they get caught up in what type of to do list to use, when, essentially the first thing to do is get into a habit of doing a to-do list.

Then slowly over time getting incrementally better, then experimenting with different To-Do list techniques.

# Create Multiple To-Do List.

To-Do Lists. Some people love them. Others hate them. I personally am a real lover of the To-Do List.

It is the best productivity Life Hack out there. Now we think that you should have multiple To-Do Lists.

As a recruiter you will have a range of balls to juggle; clients, candidates, administration, as well as managerial and internal tasks.

There are a lot of various tasks that need to be dealt with. And that does not even cover all the long-term projects that you are going to have complete at some point.

When you put this into perspective, it become less about creating multiple To-Do Lists but stopping information overload.

This is where the multiple To-Do List method comes in.

With the Multiple To-Do list Method (MTDL) you get to easily create lists that are specific for each of the balls you must juggle.

For example, as a recruiter you will need: Client, Candidate, and Administration Lists.

As a Billings Manager you will need: Client, Candidate, Administration, Managerial Lists
So how does the MTDL method work in practice?

You need to create a spreadsheet on your desktop called To Do List once created, you need to create three Columns Completed? Task, and List.

Add a filter to this row. Begin populating the spreadsheet with all the tasks that need to be completed.

On each task also put the appropriate list e.g. Candidate, Client etc.

Once you have fully populated the spreadsheet with all of your tasks that need doing you are now ready to print.

Filter the spreadsheet by each list type e.g. candidate and print off.
Take the printed copies for each of you lists and number each item 1,2,3 in order of importance.
Leave the office and go home.
Tomorrow repeat but put a Y in the Completed column against each task that you have completed. Filter. Print and Repeat.

This process each evening will give you the ultimate To-Do List and will allow you to get started straight away on your projects each morning.

Now go out and get them tiger!

# Number your to do list

Why should your number your to do list? Because Warren Buffet says so and he is close to the greatest investor in history.

However, do you need another more compelling reason?

How about it makes you more productive. Once you have gotten into the habit of creating a To Do list daily you should then start to also log each item in order of importance and impact on your recruitment desks business.

Deciding importance can be difficult, however I have found that one of the best ways to figure out and decide is look at my to do list and see what makes me the most uncomfortable.

Generally, as a rule of thumb this will be the most important task. From there, generally tasks further down the recruitment process are the most important. E.G. tasks closer to the candidate starting are generally the most important.

# KPI's are Dead, Long Live

# KPI's

Key Performance Indicators. Love them. Hate them. We all must use them. Who am I kidding, we all hate them, and would rather we did not use them.

Sadly, However, they are a necessary evil. The problem with most KPI's is that they are useless.

Why are they useless?

They are useless because generally they feed either one of two categories:

One, they are used to cover billing managers backs (or asses). Two, they do not have a real impact on the placement process.

Tracking lots of KPI's makes managers feel important, but it is nonsense to track 15 to 20 'key' performance indicators.

---

For any recruiter there are only five (we call them the famous five)

Recruitment Metrics that you need to be measured and managed.

Business Development Calls Attempted
Candidate Calls Attempted
Candidates Submitted
Interviews Arranged
Offers Received

These "famous five" are all that is truly needed to be measured.

Only measure what you can control   Feeling in control at work is liberating and a first formal foundation to recruitment success. Being out of control will only ever lead in recruitment to distress.

Distress is caused by the nasty combination of stress and/or pressure combined with a lack of control over the forces that create this stress.

When measuring your KPI's you should only focus on those that you can control, otherwise you will only be setting you and your consultants up for failure.

Peter Druker the famous management theorist once said "what gets measured, gets managed". Measuring key performance indicators that you cannot control through you own actions or actions from your team will lead to several things: increased stress and distress, apathy, system gaming or make them leave.

None of which are any good in the long term. So, what should you measure?

Controllable actions and controllable actions only. Deciding what KPI's you track are your own decision, but this is how we would track them.

1. Focus on the action taken not the outcome.

E.g. BD calls attempted rather than completed. Your consultants can control how many times they pick up the phone, but not how many times it is picked up at the other end.

2. Only focus on controllable actions that move candidates and clients towards deals, placements and fees. Anything else is vanity.

Get yourself and your consultants to focus on what you and they can control will bring increased positivity and productivity to your business.

# Plan in 90-day sprints

It is January 1st, We have all been there, and we have created a long list of new year's resolutions, life goals and plans for the up and coming year.

We want to complete them so bad.

You want to get fit, learn that language and bill bigger than you have ever billed before.

Suddenly, it is April fools day, and you look back and you feel a fool. Maybe this is the reason it is called April fools day!

You wanted to go to the gym, stop drinking and make great sales numbers. Sadly, you are back on the vodka at weekends, going to the gym once and have a cheeky vape with the other cool kids at work during lunchtime.

In short you suck at setting and keep annual goals. It is not really your fault as annual goals, although are cool and look really stylish, are rarely achieved because they do not create urgency or relevancy.

The annual goals younger brother is the 90-day sprint. The 90-day sprint is not as big as the Annual goals. It aims are not as sexy, but for some reason it is far more successful.

So how does the 90-day sprint work? Simply, it is setting a goal within a time frame that as a human we can imagine, feel, and our actions have a real and tangible impact towards completing them.

Billing £200,000 sounds like a lot, but when broken down into £50,000 a quarter it takes on a different veneer.

Want to read 52 books in a year. That sounds like a lot, but 13 in the 90 days seems manageable. Especially if a couple of them are Dan Brown novels!

How do we create a 90-day sprint? Firstly, what are your annual goals?

Write them down and figure them out. This may take some time, but it is worth figuring out.

Secondly, Pick the five most important things that you want to achieve. Thirdly, break them down into manageable chunks. For sales figures, divide it by 4.

For other goals think about the steps that need to be taken along the road of reaching that destination.

Four, write the 90-day goals out and read them to yourself daily. Five, on day 91 refer to your annual goals and re-set the next 90 day sprint.

# Walk away

For any recruitment consultant the most important mental attitude to possess in regard to your relationship with clients is the willingness to walk away if the vacancy or relationship is not going to be profitable.

Most recruiters are too scared to walk away. They are like sad little puppies when it comes to clients. They are not willing to walk away from low fees, multiple briefed agencies or client processes that are transactional.

In short they are too scared of missing the "potential fee" that they waste time, money and effort on clients that just do not deserve it. If you do learn how to walk away under the correct circumstances you find that:

You feel a greater sense of self-worth and power in relation to the client and more control over your desk and research time. Clients generally do not respect the "whorish" nature of most recruiters.

So, walking away can become a great personal USP. You will save yourself a huge amount of time that can be spent on finding clients that do meet your standards.

Now walking way does not mean being a jerk, just politely let the client know why and how they can get in touch if things change.

# Who's the MAN

Knowing who the MAN is or is not, is a vital part of modern recruitment.

However, many recruiters forget who the MAN is. So, who is THE MAN and why is it important?

The MAN stands for Money, Authority and Need. These are the three vital parts of the perfect prospect.

Money – they have the budget to write the cheque for your services.

Authority – they have the say-so to write this cheque.

Need – they have a problem that needs solving.

So why is this important? When you know a client has the money, the ability to spend that money and a problem that needs fixing you know that half the sales battle is done.

Understanding and identifying the MAN will allow you to focus your time, efforts and energy on those prospects that really matter.

# Become a Nerd

Nerds. Who needs them? Well, we all do. Nerds run the world these days. Should you become a Nerd?

Yes, yes you should. With just thirty minutes a day, you can become the office recruitment nerd within a few weeks.

How? Reading books and watching videos online. There are a whole host of ways to learn about recruitment online.

One of the best platforms to kick-start your learning process is  Ku.Dos.

Ku.Dos was created by Warren Kemp one of the leading providers of recruitment training in the UK and probably Europe.

Every module is around 30 minutes long and it covers the entire recruitment process from planning your day, all the way through to closing the deal and everything in between.

Warren is a real expert and he teaches in a way that is easy to understand and offers a lot of insight, tips, and hints that keep giving value everytime you watch the videos.

You can find Ku.dos at
https://www.kudos.training/

# Social Signatures

How many emails did you send last month? I sent according to google over 1,200 emails or roughly 60 a day. 60 emails a day!

That feels like alot. That is a lot of digital real estate that is going unbranded, which you need to capitalize on right now.

A simple way to capitalize on this real estate is too put your social links in your signatures.

A subtle and great hint for people to start following you.

The number that will click and follow will be small but adding these signatures will only take five minutes and with every email will be a chance to find a new follower or new like.

# Never forget anything,

# ever

Do you sometimes forget about things, whether it is that internet article you read, to the name of that company you saw on a drive about?

Well ladies and gentlemen some rather lovely people in Silicon Valley have created what users call their second brain. It is called Evernote and it is fantastic (I am a fanboy).

Why is Evernote such a fantastic life hack? Evernote operates on mobile, desktop, tablet and website applications that automatically syncs between all instances.

You can store just about anything, from web pages you found, to voice memos that can be created within the app.

Everything is synced and backed up to the cloud. Every note can be added to folders that can be shared and synced with teams.

As a recruiter, I use Evernote to store all my accounting and expenses, articles that i may want to read later and content/copy that I am creating so it can be shared straight away.

I also use the scannable feature to take paper straight to a digital format.

I could spend days writing about the brilliance of this app, my suggestion is to download it and then discover its multitude of features and go from there.

To join the Evernote revolution visit - http://evernote.com (and it is free for the light version)

# Automate Like a Boss

Want to Automate like a Boss? IFTT is like a second employee working for you in the background to help you do things between apps.

It is simple to use and can really save you loads of time and effort on simple repetitive tasks. Fancy having every LinkedIn post sent to Twitter?

IFTT can help with that. Want your website's blog automatically posted to Facebook?

IFTT can do that. Want to save an email automatically to Evernote, IFTT can do that. Been sent an attachment?

IFTT can save it straight to your GDrive. IFTT can automatically do a wide range of things from everything like putting your android phone on mute when you reach work to logging your time on devices, apps and websites.

This really is only scratching the surface. This is just a taste of the all the Apps that use it. Everyone from Amazon to Philips and Dominos are on the platform.

How it works is by creating Applets, and every day thousands of new Applets are created by users.

So, if there is something that you want to do, the chances are that someone else will have already created it. Once you start using it, it does start to become addictive.

For instance, I get an email every day that tells me the weather and I also share a random Wikipedia articles to my personal Facebook, why? just for fun really.

IFTT can save you time and hassle. Set aside a couple of hours on a Friday to find out more.

To explore and save time go to http://iftt.com If you are into hardcore automation, you may want to try http://zapier.com

# Set and Forget Social

Does Tweeting, Facebooking, LinkedIn-ing (is that a word?) and Instagramming seem to take up alot of your time?

I bet it does.

Each day going onto twitter etc is a time thief. Before you know it you are watching a Thomas the Tank engine/Beyonce mash up for the first time and somehow it is 11am.

These platforms are designed to be addictive, the longer you are on them the more advertising revenue they get.

So beat the social giants at their own game by using Buffer. Buffer is a brilliant little package which is cloud, website and app based. Buffer allows you to schedule social media output ahead of time so that you can batch the tasks and then get on with your day.

Buffer works by allowing you to decide how many posts to do a day, what time to send them and then allows you to fill up these slots ahead of time.

Buffer also gives you real time analytics on how the posts are doing and saves previous posts so they can be shared again in the future if they did well.

Buffer's usefulness does not end there. You can also install a Buffer plugin or the app on Apple products and automatically put useful articles into your scheduled queue.

Buffer also have a host of other features that are worth exploring at http://buffer.com

# Keep your social

# Evergreen

Do you ever just seem to be posting the same updates on to social media every week? Does it feel like you are just wasting time?

Well, the chances are you are. Want to save this time for things more important like online shopping or watching videos of cats. I bet you do.

Then you should get Recurrpost the best partner to use with Buffer. So why is Recurrpost such a Life Hack?

It will recycle your best content on Facebook, twitter, linked and Instagram again and again on the day and time that suit you and your audience.

You can even set up RSS feeds, so they automatically get shared and shared again. This life hack will really save you time and will help you automatically build those audiences.

You will have to invest a lot of time upfront, but once you have invested the time upfront it will save you time each day of the week, forever onwards.

# Keep up to date and share

# with Feedly

Do you want to keep up with all the best developments in your area of expertise?

Of course, you do.

Do you want to have your blogs, newspapers and YouTube videos all in one place?

You bet you do.

Do you want to share this with all your contacts? That sounds like a third yes to me. This is where Feedly can and does step in.

Feedly allows you to aggregate and discover content from across the web all in one place on your phone or iPad.

The brilliance of this App means that when you are on the bus or tube into work you can find four or five articles that your audience will love and then get on with the rest of your day, safe in the knowledge your audience is catered for. Now if you know how to use RSS feeds, Zapier or IFTT Feedly becomes a piece of genius. Use this Applet from IFFT and every time you find an interesting article on Feedly it will automatically be added to your Buffer social queue.

Quick and easy thought leadership social media at the touch of a button. Feedly is located at https://feedly.com/

Read a book an hour

Do you sometimes feel it takes too long to get to the good stuff from a business or self-help book? I do.

Sometimes the great ideas are just surrounded by waffle. Blinklist cures this problem in a handy app that is for both iPhone and Android. Blinklist will allow you to digest a book in a lunchtime.

Blinklist cuts books and audiobooks down into short article or audio snippets that cover the key learning points from the text. It really is a wonderful concept. They have a wide range of titles.

Almost any decent non-fiction book will be on there. So why is this a life hack?

You can use Blinklist to turbocharge your learning on a subject in a very quick time. Imagine having all the key points from Adam Smiths Wealth of Nations read to you whilst on your commute to work?

Or when you are eating lunch taking onboard the teachings of Anthony Robbins. Imagine what listening to all the best sales books would do for your daily calling and sales figures?

It may not be the entire book, but you get the best, juiciest bits. Blinklist does the hard work for you.

You can find Blinklist in the App store or at https://www.blinkist.com We suggest you start with this list of books on Blinklist

# Reduce Internal Emails

# with Slack

Internal emails. Internal mind farts normally. How many times do you end up sending emails like text messages?

More often than you care to admit. And even if you do not, I bet you can think of someone who does.
So what is the cure for dealing with all these internal emails? Smashing up everyone's PC's? That might work.

Although a P45 may end up in the post. What is more likely to work would be moving internal communication to Slack or Facebook For Work.

Both programmes are essentially instant messenger services or chat programmes, but for work (so no eggplant emoji's).

The beauty of both platforms is that they have been developed specifically for teams to work together, cut email and smooth out communication.

There may be some internal resistance to moving away from 100% email.

However, the gains to be had are mind blowing!

Slack can be found at www.slack.com

Facebook for Work can be found at www.facebook.com workplace

# One Software Package to

# rule them all

This hack is aimed at the business owner, decision maker and solo recruiter (shout out to all the solo recruitment hero's!).

If you want to save time and money on your software needs, you cannot get better than Zoho One. Depending on what your requirements are Zoho One pretty much has it covered.

For a small yearly payment, you get everything from a CRM, ATS, Accounts, Expenses and Checkout package, Website designer, social media aggregator, email marketing platform and about 30 other programs.

You save time by only have to renew once a year. At the time of publication, the Zoho One package cost circa £330/$500 and that is for everything. For the year!

Check out Zoho One at
https://www.zoho.com/one

# Find (almost) any email address with Hunter.io

Tracking down emails whilst researching prospects and candidates can be a time-consuming process and sometimes all you can do is really just guess.

We have all done this guessing game and it is a pain. Hunter.io solves this problem. Hunter.io is a Chrome extension and a website that searches and stores emails from the across the internet for almost every and any company.

The joy of Hunter is that if it finds an email, it tells you the source, plus, also recommends possible formats for those it does not have.

You can use a Hunter as a bog standard webpage. Where it really comes into its own is the Chrome extension.

You are on joebloggsaccountants.com and want to find emails addresses, click on the Hunter icon and it will bring up all the emails found associated with this web address.

Like lightning, it is there. Brilliant, simple, effective. You can find Hunter at https://hunter.io/

# Keep Calm and Carry on

# with Calm

Anyone who tells you recruitment is not stressful is either a liar or not a recruiter. Recruitment is one of the most stressful careers there is. Why? Because 100% of your product is basically dealing with people, and we all know how stressful people are.

This is where Calm can come in and be a really helpful source of chill in a sea of craziness. Calm was voted the best App of 2017, which is to be fair an amazing accolade.

What Calm does is threefold of brilliance.

1) It offers guided meditations around a range of topics and issues from keeping calm to building your confidence to dealing with anxiety.
2) It has calming and mellow stories that are both inspirational and great as adult bedtime stories.

3) It also offers calming music that can be anything from rainforest sounds to waterfalls so that you can zone out from the hustle and bustle and find some inner peace. I like putting on the ambient music when I have to focus, or I am a little stressed during a hard day.

You can find Calm at https://www.calm.com

# Hire your own Grammar

# Nazi

Time for me to be vulnerable.

One of my biggest weaknesses is my Dyslexia (I found later in life it is a massive strength). As a child, I was told I was unlikely to get any GCSE's let alone go to University.

In time the weakness become my biggest strength because I turned it into motivation that led me ultimately to gain a Masters Degree from Aberdeen Graduate Business School. However, overall it was a massive struggle to dealing with spelling, punctuation and grammar.

If only I had something like Grammarly. Grammarly is basically your own grammar nazi sitting on your computer showing you what you have done wrong.

It has free and paid for versions. I use the free version (via a chrome plugin) and I find it far more useful than inbuilt spelling and grammar checkers.

It is a Chrome and Internet Explorer plugin which means that it will check anything that you type on a webpage, social media, or within Gmail.

Which is a brilliant way to keep everything tip-top and spelt correctly. This really is a game changer as it means you do not have to leave applications to check for those pesky spelling, punctuation and grammar mistakes.

You can find Grammarly at
https://www.grammarly.com

# Sail off into the sunset

# with Anchor

Personally, I love a good podcast, it is exciting learning from some of the world greatest business and self-help minds.

From Tim Ferris to Anthony Robbins to the Renegade Recruiter, they all have insights that I personally think add real value to my day job. Now you can join these giants and launch your own podcast in minutes and have episodes up on Apple podcasts in just 48 hours.

All with your phone or tablet and that's all. How may you ask, can you achieve this feat? With the Anchor app.

Anchor is an Android and Apple App that harnesses the power of your phone and some computer wizardry to help you launch your very own podcast.

Your phone has an amazing microphone with noise reduction technology that makes it a perfect recording station.

Anchor uses this to help you record podcasts. And it gets better, you record as if you are having a telephone conversation meaning that you can record whilst sitting at your desk and then edit and publish all from your phone.

It even has jingles! I am really blown away by this App. Keep your eyes peeled for a Podcast soon.

You can find Anchor on the App store and Android marketplace as well as at https://anchor.fm/

# The Best Email Habit –

Always Process to Inbox Zero whenever you go onto your emails you should always process them to zero. Don't let anything else get in the way of processing them to zero. Zero is your goal.

This one habit will help tame your inbox and will free up your day to do important things like organizing the drinks after work on a Friday or prospecting for new clients.

You know important stuff. Below I have outlined a workflow you can use to process emails and get inbox to inbox zero.

1. Open email.

2. Read email.

3. Is action required? Y or N.

4. If Yes, will this action take less than two minutes?

If yes, do straight away.

If no, add to Action folder.

5. If no action is required does the email need to go into a folder?

Yes - Add to Folder.

No - Read the email then delete if unimportant or archive for later reference.

Use this above workflow until you have cleared your inbox entirely then do three 45-minute email bursts a day from then on. You will have taken control of your inbox and will feel very free afterwards.

# Batch Emails and then

# turn them off

All emails are super important, and you need to respond to them straight away said no successful person ever. Emails like almost all tasks should be scheduled and batched into specific times each day. Why should you do this? Emails are not that important and in 99.999999999% of the time they can wait a couple of hours.

It is just control freak culture that keeps us checking emails, every five minutes of the day. The benefits of batching emails are threefold:

Firstly: By batching your emails into slots e.g. 9am, 1pm and 4:30pm you can focus the rest of the day on the important tasks like business development calls and networking with candidates.

Secondly: You do not lose cognitive focus by switching between tasks. As you switch between tasks it can take up to ten minutes to get the brain into gear for the new task. That is alot of wasted brain power and focus.

Thirdly: By having your emails batched at specific times you are saying to yourself I am the master of my time and the captain of my inbox.

Now if you must send a client or candidate a quick email you really should do it through the CRM or ATS if they have this functionality.

This will stop the temptation to deal with other emails and will also keep them tracked as well. Because if it is not tracked, it is not fact!

# Candidate Application

# Emails

This is a super quick hack. When processing your emails and you get an application from a candidate put it into a separate application folder. Why?

So you can batch processing candidate CV's and applications quickly and from one location onto your ATS.

This way you will not have to scramble around and will be able to quickly and efficiently deal with them without them clogging up your inbox.

# Quick, simple and effective. Ignore or 'call out' useless emails

You do not need to be CC'd into the latest of 350 birthday card emails that circulate around the company at any one time. Call them out as time wasting.

Or do what I did when I worked at a large company, I put emails from timewasters under a set rule which put them into a folder called timewasters.

You may occasionally miss something, but generally Stacy's email about David's birthday in the Colchester office will not be worth reading. Unless you are David in the Colchester office.

I may sound like an old fart, however, so much time is wasted by these emails it makes my blood boil. If you do decide to call out the time-wasting emailer do it carefully and with tact.

Do not say "Sharon this is b******t, stop sending this stuff about the 'buy a cake from the supermarket and pretend you baked it' day."

Instead, say. "Thank you for keeping us all posted on the upcoming bake sale in aid of injured seagulls, however, could I be left off in future as I get a lot of emails each day and I would like to lower my email burden to ensure I am tip-top for my candidates and clients. I hope you understand."

Remember it is your time and your inbox not Sharon's.

# Templates of the Gods

Do you feel like you write the same emails time and time again? The chances are without even realising it, you are sending dozens maybe even hundreds of emails a week that are basically the same. What a waste of time, life, and energy. Templates are really a gift from the gods when it comes to emails.

Now depending on your email system, it can be easy or hard to have easy to access templates. I personally use the GSuite application - Inbox by Google which has a handy template feature making it really simple to create and send templates. If you are using another programme like outlook, then this is a little trickier, but can easily be done.

Whatever programme you are using, creating email templates is a brilliant way to respond to emails quickly, and create world-class responses that just take a click of a button. We suggest you make templates for the following situations below (I am sure you can come up with more ideas).

Candidate Submission Email to Client Candidate

Submission Confirmation to Candidate

Interview Confirmation - Client Interview
Confirmation - Candidate Interview
Confirmation - Meeting You Rejection Email

Rejection Email - Can you call me back Terms of

Business Email Client Invoice Email Client

Payment Chasing Letter One Client Payment

Chasing Letter Two Client Payment Chasing

Final Letter chasing payment.

Once one person has created these emails
templates if you share them with your team the
time-saving life hacking with be massive.

# Always call first, email

# second

You are a recruiter; the phone is your natural habitat.

You are a lion and the phone is your African savannah.

Email is the Atlantic Ocean. Do you see many Lions in the Sea? Okay, smart ass in the back, yes there are sea lions, but you do not often see them hunting and catching Zebra. So call, call, call.

Always call before emailing a candidate, client or colleague, it will speed up the processing of emails and tasks. Likely get you a better result compared to sending an email. How can you make this work daily to really hack productivity?

What if you do not get through to the person or need an audit trail?

Calling instead of emailing will really boost your productivity as you will, in a 2-minute call, be able to communicate and make progress on a wide range of tasks that would have taken a long time to send, respond, negotiate and agree via emails.

When calling someone if you do not get through, leave them a voicemail and then send them a quick email saying I have left a voicemail responding to this or send the email you were going to send. If you need an audit trail, then after a call, just send a quick summing up email that will cover (your ass) as an audit trail.

Of course, if something is very important write an email, but for 95% to 99% a quick call rather than email will suffice.

# Just Unsubscribe

Do you get a lot of emails?

Marketing and round-robin type emails.

Do they waste a lot of time?

Let's be honest I bet you have loads. I do. So just be ruthless on your next Inbox Zero mission and click unsubscribe.

Be ruthless, especially with anything that is vaguely personal in nature as each email with kill your time.

For example, if you get Wowcher or other similar emails. If that email takes up one minute a day across a year you have just wasted 6 hours of your life on bargains on toilet rolls and garden lights.

Save this stuff for your personal email and just hit unsubscribe. Unsubscribe.   Unsubscribe. Unsubscribe.

# Do not ask for Permission

# via email

Sometimes it feels like emails can be used like instant messenger chatroom from the late 1990's. Ping, email. Ping, email. Ping, email. If you use the correct language you can reduce and eliminate all these small time-wasting emails that take up your day.

You can do this by not asking for permission in emails.

So what do we mean?

How can not asking for permission reduce the number of emails you receive?

Simply, asking for permission means that the other person has to both think through the decision and then communicate that decision to you normally in another email.

So instead of asking for permission why not just say what you are going to do, at a specific time. We will give an example below to demonstrate what we mean.

Asking for Permission: Hello Dave, attached is the Press Release written about the new product launch. Can you read it for me. If it is okay, can I send the Press Release to News and Stuff? Regards, Sarah

Going Ahead without permission: Hello Dave, attached is the Press Release for the product launch. It is ready to be sent. Please read the attachment. We are going to send it to News and Stuff at three PM if we do not hear from you about any further changes. Regards, Sarah.

Do you see what we mean? By not asking for permission you are giving yourself and the other person the chance to save time, energy and space in the inbox.

# Your Inbox, Your Rules

The Inbox is not your master, it is your inbox, so you make the rules.

You can master the inbox, you can create your own rules. Around the globe slavery was abolished for the most part over 100 years ago. However, for many people in their offices today, the 'inbox' has become a virtual slave master creating tons of stress and destroying productivity.

However, you can change this relationship by developing rules that mean the inbox works for you. But you have to create these rules and stick by them.

Personally, I use these three rules when dealing with my inbox.

1) Process all emails until you hit inbox zero three times a day first thing, lunchtime and before heading home.
2) Read any emails that need to be read at this minute and archive or delete straight away.

3) Work to Inbox zero then start on my to-do list. These rules work for me.

However, they may not work for you. If you are struggling to create your own rules what we suggest is that you sit down away from your email and brainstorm what is important and what is not important with emails in regard to you key priorities.

Once you have done that. Pick the three rules that you think will improve your daily battle with the inbox and stick to them rigidly for 28 days and see what happens.

Have a calendar item booked in for the 29th day to review how it worked and what you may need to change.

# Move to GSuite

Google. You cannot beat these guys and gals. They really do an amazing job at whatever they do.

From having the greatest search engine ever created to the whole host of applications for free or a tiny price.

The most important product in this is GSuite and notably their email function. Inbox by Google (a special Gmail feature) is easily the best way to deal with emails on the internet today. Move over Microsoft and your old school Outlook. Why is Google's Inbox so good? Five clear reasons?

1) Simple archiving and the power of Google search for your emails.
2) Tasks can be created in the Inbox that means using it as a workflow tool is simple.
3) Cloud-based so can be loaded on Phones, Tablets, and Browsers so easy access anywhere.

4) Can snooze emails for a given time so that they stay out of sight and out of mind.
5) Stripped back design, simplicity is the key here and it is wonderful.

These functions can also be enhanced with a wide range of plugins that an outlook would kill for. Want to add data to your CRM?

There will be a plugin for that. Want to see if people have opened the message? There will be a plugin for that too.

You can find Inbox at http://inbox.google.com and G-Suite at https://gsuite.google.co.uk/

# Holiday Emails are the Devil

Do you find that you are checking your emails whilst you are on holiday?

It is a sin that is now pervasive and damaging. Checking emails whilst on holiday is the worst of all worlds.

You cannot properly action the email, but you also cannot forget about it. It leaves you in a world of anguish, annoyance or stress.

Those two weeks in the sun are hard won, expensive and are there to help you unwind, they should not be ruined by emails that your colleagues could deal with. So here is our life hack to deal with holiday emails.

Delete them.

That's right delete them as soon as you get back into the office. Okay, it does go deeper than this but, before you leave for holiday you should reach inbox zero. Process your inbox to zero.

Deal with every email, if it requires an action put it onto your to do list. Then once you have done this delete the Email apps and other email services from your phone and iPad.

Once this has been done you then put on an out of office on that says the following:

*"Thank you for your email. I appreciate the time that you have taken to email me. Currently, I am on annual leave and will not be checking my emails. This email will be deleted and will go unread. I will be returning on the xxxx at Midday. Please reshedule the message to send for then or if it is urgent please call xxxxx xxxxx and ask for xxxxx. Thank you for understanding."*

When you get back into the office, delete every email that is sat in your Inbox.

Now I know as you read this you are horrified by the prospect of deleting emails. What if you miss something?

I would bet my last dollar, rupee or penny that you would not miss anything and if it is really, urgent then they will call your office anyway. The out of office will have made that clear and if it is important your client or candidate will have to call into the office.

Follow this hack and you will have a more tranquil holiday.

# Research and Use Plugins

Email is email right. Wrong.

Email with plugins can be brilliant, fantastic even.

You can tell I am excited by all this! Why are plugins such a brilliant thing?

Time saving. Time saving. Time saving. Depending on which software packages you use and which email suite you have there are a whole host of plugins that can work wonders.

For instance, I use Zoho, which has a Gmail plugin that allows you to enter data straight into the CRM, saving loads of time and effort. For GSuite I have used the Boomerang plugin that allows you to time when you send and email and stop emails coming into your inbox.

On Outlook in the past I have used the Bullhorn and Evernote plugins. Google "Gmail Plugins" or "Outlook Plugins" to find some of the best plugins on the market.

# Turn those emails off

# Emails.

The constant ping, ping, ping of new messages. We are as a society addicted to the things.

Especially in recruitment, we do not seem to be able to switch them off. We keep looking at them "just in case".

However, "just in case" never really happens. Emails are important but during core business development hours we really should be turning these emails off.

To many in recruitment, this will be very, very uncomfortable.

However, when you are talking to a candidate about their next career steps or a client about that important and vital hire, should you be distracted by emails?

No of course not. Having a clear focus on one task - in this case making calls, will improve your results and give you more important things to email your boss about, like more deals.

So how can you turn your emails off and not get it in the ear from your boss or clients?

1) Close your email and just get on with your important tasks and see if anyone notices.
2) Create a simple out of office reminder that says:

*"Thank you for your email. Between 10:00 - 12:00 and 14:00 - 17:00 I am serving my clients and candidates and will not be on my emails. If your request is urgent please call my direct line on xxxxx"*

You will be amazed at just how rarely the email is as urgent as you think they are. Try it, go on, dare you! Triple dare you!

# Hoot, Hoot, HootSuite

You have messages coming into you from every man and his dog on Twitter, Facebook, Instagram, LinkedIn and Pinterest.

This is a problem and really can take up loads of time. Hootsuite can solve this issue almost instantly.

HootSuite allows you to post, share and engage in comment conversations right on the one platform.

It saves you time and makes conversations and comments easy to manage and avoids the time killing death spiral that is cat videos.

You can find HootSuite at https://hootsuite.com

# Recycling is good

Recycling is good. It is very hard to argue with this, although I am sure the internet will provide someone to argue with me.

However, when it comes to social media recycling it is even more awesome as it can be automated, thus saving you time and allowing all your followers the chance to love the content all over again.

Recycling social media updates is great as generally with most feeds on social media only 10-20% of your audience will get the update in their feed, and only around half might look at it. So resharing will increase the chance that they will see it and love it.

If you are going to go down the "recycling" social route we suggest that you do two things:
1) Create content that is evergreen and does not age
2) Use Edgar Edgar is a lovely little Octopus that will share and reshare your content on a fixed schedule time and time again.

It is wonderfully easy to use and given the time saved is great value for money.

The premise is simple. Create updates e.g. sharing a blog post.

Set when these updates are to go out and hit publish. Your updates will be recycled time and time again.

Want to update Twitter about Taco Tuesdays? Now you can update everyone and spend more time eating Tacos.

You can meet the friendly social sharing Octopus at https://meetedgar.com/

# Cross Platform promotion

When on Twitter you should promote your Facebook page.

When on YouTube you should promote your Twitter.

When on Instagram you should promote you Facebook page. You get the idea.

When you are on social media you really want to at least once a week to promote all your other social accounts and media channels.

This cross-platform promotion will do several things:

1) It will give you content to share - new YouTube video go and share it on Twitter etc. Once you have shared it, it will create likes on that platform and increases followers on the other platform.

2) As more people follow you across different social account it will grow your reach and allow you to be as a welcome source of useful and career changing information.
3) If your focus, for the next six months is on building your Twitter following, it means you can leverage this twitter following to build a well-liked and followed Facebook page later.
4) It will help you understand who your true fans are and allow you to market towards similar people via paid advertising.
5) Reduces your reliance on one platform because who knows one day Twitter may go bust. Or Facebook makes changes that affect your reach.

In light of my own advice, you can follow me on Twitter and Facebook.

# Creepy Facebook

Would you like to easily and simply retarget prospects on Facebook with highly relevant adverts after they have visited your webpage?

Of course, you do.

This is how Facebook Pixel comes in and can a real benefit to you. Facebook Pixel is a tiny bit of code that will 'follow' a visitor to your website around the internet and allow you to serve clever retargeting campaigns.

It sounds a bit creepy, but it is very effective, and the chances are you have been retargeted in such a manner by numerous websites and businesses over the years.

So how could you use this to increase your social media following?

A candidate visits your jobs page and with the Facebook pixel you can follow them around Facebook with either adverts to follow your company page or serve up job adverts to them. There are numerous ways you can use this.

It is very effective and slightly creepy!

# Think Value

When Engaging in social media what you want to be focusing on is providing value.

We have been there, we follow a page or a twitter account because we think it will be great, however, all you get is spammed with some of the worst, useless stuff and before long you have unfollowed.

What was going on here, was simply the owner of the page or twitter handle was thinking about themselves rather than their audience. Serve to your audience first, sell second.

So when it comes to social media, before you post anything you have to ask yourself, does this provide real value to my audience? A no, silence or an umm, will probably tell all the story that you need to know.

So do not share.

So what does generally add value to your audience?

Essentially this will come down to who is in your audience and what you specialise in recruitment wise.

Things that add real value are always career advice, hiring advice and industry news.

# Understand Social

# Algorithms

Algorithms are mentioned alot in the press and media, but, generally people misunderstand what they are.

At times they have become a digital "boogyman", being responsible for all sorts of misdeeds. However, in all things knowledge is power and the truth is generally in the details.

So what is an algorithm?

According to the lovely people at Techopedia.com

*"An algorithm is a step by step method of solving a problem. It is commonly used for data processing, calculation and other related computer and mathematical operations.   An algorithm is also used to manipulate data in various ways, such as inserting a new data item, searching for a particular item or sorting an item."*

So when it comes to all social media feeds there is an algorithm that will solve the "problem" of what updates and content to put into your feed. For sharing and being successful on social media this is a vital thing to understand.

As an example, Facebook, LinkedIn and Instagram are all currently, at the date of publication, using their algorithms to promote video content and paid for content over organic pictures and text posts.

This means if you share a video on LinkedIn, it will be more likely to appear in the feeds of your audience over just a plain text post.

Do your research and think about how you will engage and post on social media in the future.

# Value Not Volume

When it comes to social media we all get bored of the rubbish content some people share. We have all been there with someone who posts absolute rubbish.

However, if we really want to have an impact on social media we need to think value not volume. So what do we mean by value?

Value is what is valuable to your audience e.g. candidates and clients. Nothing else matters. What interests your clients and your candidates are all that matters.

Ask them, and then act up on it! Less can be more

This is a repeat of the last hack. Less can be more, especially if it adds real value. Enough said.

# Stay off social

I could go into this in real depth and detail, but essentially, you don't want to be posting onto social media directly.

Why?

Because when you go onto these platforms they are designed to entice you into spending time on the platform and you do not want to spend your working life on Facebook. Social Media creates a mini-high from dopamine (the happy/addict chemical) every time you scroll down your social feed.

Every comment and like recreates this mini hit. This is what you want to avoid as it will eat into your recruitment hours and only make Mark Zuckerberg richer.

So, to avoid this, post onto these platforms using Buffer, Hootsuite or Tweetdeck.

So, kids, stay of social (that sounds like a rubbish anti-drugs slogan from the 1990's).

# The Pomodoro Technique

The Pomodoro technique is named after a kitchen tomato timer, of all things, that was invented by an Italian chap. And essentially, it's a productivity tool that is simple, straightforward, and it's really, quite effective.

What you're doing is you batch your time into 25-minute slots called a Pomodoro, and in that slot, you focus on one thing and one task only and nothing else.

During that 25 minutes, that's all you focus on, either until you have completed the task or the timer goes off. When the Pomodoro goes off and it rings the bell, you take a 5- to 10-minute break, get away from your desk, then you come back and you do another Pomodoro.

You just keep repeating like that all day. What this technique does is it sets an artificial barrier of time, it blocks everything else out, and it focuses you through creating a sense of urgency.

And it's brilliant. And the great thing is if someone is coming to disturb you, all you do is say, "Can you come to me at the end of Pomodoro?

There's about 10 minutes left." And then you continue. It's great. Use it. I use it. This book was written using this very hack!

# Batch tasks

Do all of one type of task, at one time, in one big batch.

Why?

Because it's more efficient. If you have to process candidate's registration meetings and calls onto the system, do it once a day or week.

Why?

By switching between tasks, it can take up to 10 minutes to 15 minutes for the brain to switch into gear for that new task, which means that you will probably either take longer or will do the job poorly.

So if you meet 10 candidates in a week, on the Friday afternoon, set yourself an hour to put all their details on the system, bish bash bosh, and in an hour, you get all their details onto the system.

You've saved yourself a lot of time, but also, as you put their details on the system at the same time, you'll be consistent in the way that you do it because you'll be following the same process.

Although it means that your stats won't necessarily be updated day to day on that type of thing, over a weekly basis, batching matters and will have a big impact.

You should batch your BD calls. You should batch LinkedIn time. You should batch your emails. Batching should be part of your daily business.

# Go Dark

No this is not about going all James Bond. However, sometimes you literally just must go dark.

You must turn off everything. You must turn off your phone, you have to turn off your email, and you have to get on with work. You must ignore the notifications.

Now, in recruitment, ignoring communication and telephone calls has always been a bit of a sin, almost a heresy in some circles. But I for one believe that if you're always responding, you are not being responsible.

So sometimes you must go dark to focus on those important tasks and use the going dark method to essentially make important decisions.

Say for instance you must decide on a software purchase between two suppliers. Say it's for an Application Tracking System.

Now you've gone over all the details and what you do is you go dark. You take the details. You turn off your phone. You turn off your internet, everything. You go through the decision for a certain amount of time, say 25 minutes.

Once that time has ended, you make a firm decision. That's how going dark can be used for decisions.

Additionally, if you have work to do that is not based on communicating with people, going dark is a great way of getting it done quickly and getting back on with other subjects.

# Have sales hours for

# specific campaigns

Each week, you can dedicate a certain amount of your sales hours to specific types of calls and specific types of campaigns.

The reason why you should do this is to keep diversity in the calls that you make.

To ensure that you are covering all the bases with your calls, but also so that you do not do the same type of call day in, day out.

With the variety, you will get better at the calls. You will sound more interested, more engaged, and the clients will hear that in your voice and your passion will come across.

# Work-life balance is a

# myth

The people who talk about work-life balance and are tell you how amazing it is.

How important and vital it is, and how if you do not have work-life balance you are a failure are probably:

1) Lying or
2) Selling you courses or books on work-life balance. There is no balance.

There never will be balance because work is important and so is family life.

Balance means that neither receives the focus they deserve. Sometimes it will get out of kilter. And that's why what you'll want to do is you fit your work into your lifestyle and vice-versa.

How I've done that is I've worked for myself, meaning that I can fit my work around my life and my life around my work.

If you're working for a big corporate, this will never happen. They may talk about work-life balance, but, everything is geared towards work and not your life.

So, if you want to create a life that's worth living and engaging with, work for yourself so you can integrate your work into your life.

# Have Stand Up Meetings

The meeting has now entered its 365th hour and Janice from procurement has asked you a question and you realize that you are not paying attention and that you have been slumped in your chair, you totally zoned out.

Why did you zone out? Because the meeting has gone on for a very long time, mainly because everyone is comfortably sat down.

The cure to long, meandering meetings is to hold 'stand up meetings'. Although there maybe some resistance to the idea of a stand-up meeting, it really is a wonderful innovation to bring into the workplace.

Every meeting will be quicker, more effective and will end up in more decisions being taken. These are wonderful benefits to have. So why are standing up meetings better?

When everyone is stood up it puts people in a more 'action' ordinated mindset because as cavemen or cavewomen we would have been standing up to do all the important action focused things like hunting and wrestling with sabre tooth tigers.

By standing up this mindset will come into play during meetings. When you are standing up your voice sounds different and you talk at a quicker pace, everyone in the room having the meeting will talk at a quicker punchier pace.

Wafflers generally will want to get the meeting over, so they can sit down again at their desk and waffle to their work neighbor.

A standing meeting is also healthy as most recruiters spend a good portion of their day on the phone at their desk sitting on their bums. Sitting is the new smoking and has huge health risks so everyone will benefit.

So, the next time Janice wants a meeting to discuss paperclip purchases recommend a quick stand up meeting.

# No Agenda, No Meeting

Have you ever been in a meeting and it felt like a total waste of time. We have all been there, the meeting where Keith from Accounts mutters on for ages, Jenny from Marketing talks and talks and talks and talks and after 90 minutes another meeting is booked in the diary without anything being accomplished.

It is a total waste of life and could be time that you had spent on prospective clients.

As Dave Barry once described meetings as:
*"Meetings are an addictive, highly self-indulgent activity that corporations and other large organizations habitually engage in only because they cannot actually masturbate."*

Which is a tad rude, however he really does capture the sentiment behind all the wasted times in meetings.

So, what is a great way to ensure that you only have meetings that are productive? Ensure that every meeting has an agenda. Now, within some organisations this will be harder to accomplish that others, but quite simply, decline any meeting that does not have an agenda.

That way you will avoid those meetings that are destined to be time wasters. If you cannot avoid the meeting due to this excuse simply create the agenda. That way you will look professional and will keep the meeting on track.

All agendas should only have three points   I've covered this in another life hack about why you should never have a meeting without an agenda. Now, in this one, we discuss why every agenda should only have three points.

That's all you need. Three points. The three points are the problem, the discussion of the solutions, and then the decision on the solution and who is accountable.

So essentially three points. What is the problem? What are the potential solutions?  What is the decision? Who will implement?

So, it's the problem, it's the solution, it's the decision. That way, you go in with a formulated problem that everyone's got to discuss, you come up together with a solution, and then you make the decision on which solution is best and who is accountable.

That way, you get an efficient meeting and you're there to talk about moving things forward instead of just having a conversation.

# Stand up and be counted

When on the telephone, one of the best ways to get a better outcome is to stand up when making calls. You might think that you look an idiot standing up whilst everyone in the office is sitting down.

However, your results will soon speak for themselves come pay day. Standing up when on the phone is like magic for a whole number of reasons.

Firstly, it changes the shape of your body, meaning, the sounds you make when talking are different and people on the other end of the line can tell and will react in a positive way. They will indeed hear your height!

Secondly, in relation to the phone on your desk you will be taller, so you will feel more confident as you will be bigger and taller than the phone. Although this seems like madness, remember we are all chimps at the end of the day.

Thirdly, standing up creates confidence as you will be standing up straight and have your shoulders out, meaning you are not slumped at your desk.

The last and best reason? It is so much healthier than sitting down for eight, nine, or ten hours day.

Remember Donald Rumsfeld used a standing desk and look at everything he accomplished.

Oh.

# Catch candidates

# everytime

Ring, ring, ring, ring, voicemail.

How many times does this happen to you when calling candidates. Loads I bet, as it happens loads with me as well.

A quick and simple way to reduce the amount of time wasted like this is too get candidates to book directly into your calendar.

This means when you pick up the phone they are at the other end of the line reading and waiting.

This is a timesaver and gives a really good impression to the candidates about how professional you are.

So how can you do this?

Personally, I use Acuity Scheduler to do this as it is simple, easy and cheap.

Once you have created your profile all you need to do then is set the times you are free to speak each week and send the link generated to candidates to book in the call.

You can find Acuity by Googling Acuity Scheduler

# Use a script

Now, most people think only actors should use them, but I for one think scripts are brilliant. I think whether you're making a candidate speccing call or you're doing a routine introductory BD call, you should definitely use a script.

You should always have a scriptbook to hand. Even if you don't use it, scripts are basically your get out of jail card.

What I mean, if something is going wrong, you can refer to them and keep a call on track. Additionally, they're a confidence booster because they create a safety net and that safety net will make you more confident. And thirdly, scripts give a systematic process for making a call.

You follow the same process in every call. You start to see where it works, where it doesn't work, and how you are working at being effective that day, that week or month.

It allows you to standardize your process, but also for you to measure your success as well.

# Smile Before You Dial

This life hack I feel wins the award for being the cheesiest hack in the entire book. Do not worry, I heard your groans, but please do keep with me on this.

Smile when you dial is a cliché and as with alot of clichés people in this cynical internet age ignore them because they are after all quite awkward and embarrassing.

Something becomes a cliché because there is a real element of truth to it, and when it comes to smiling as you dial the truth is very much there. Smiling when you dial does a number of things that will help you as you are making calls.

1) When you are smiling people can hear this in your voice and you will sound more appealing and persuasive on the phone.
2) When you make the muscle movements that form a smile it releases happiness chemicals that will make you feel happier and if you feel happier you will perform better on the phone.

3) When it becomes a habit that is repeated and repeated as you smile before you dial the body will automatically become hardwired into a positive state.

Thank you for bearing with me through the cheese!

# Get past the gatekeeper

# with "Thank you"

Gatekeepers, they're a real pain. They could be a real pain for anyone. As a recruiter, I of course find them very, very annoying because they're stopping you from getting in contact with the people who I can help most: hiring managers.

That's their job, sadly. And for what it's worth, they do a good job and we should thank them.

What you should do is you should thank them. When you are asking at a gatekeeper for a person (the gatekeeper could be a receptionist or whoever picks up the phone), say the person's name and then just say "Thank you" and be silent.

The amount of times this works is amazing because essentially no one likes silence, and the longer the silence goes on, the more likely they are going to take the easy option to end the silence, which is to say, "Putting you through."

So next time you're at a gatekeeper, say "Thank you." It will do a world of difference.

# Have two questions

Whenever you are on a business development call, you need to have two questions for every single prospect.

Having two questions will triple the number of chances you get to build a relationship with a client. Now, these two questions, they can be on anything recruitment or industry related. The first one should be the recruitment-focused outcome you are looking for.

For example, you want to get the job-on with the client who been advertising for a that role you have seen.

So you do the whole lead chasing bog standard recruitment question. And like the Chumba-Wumba song, you get knocked down. However, you can get right back up again because you have a second question.

The second question can be more creative. If you are looking to play it safe something that is industry-related that you can use to help market to them in the future.

Below we have outlined a mini-script to demonstrate what we mean.

YOU: "Hello, Mr. Client. Can I help you with this job?"

CLIENT: "No." YOU: "One more question before I go. What are your thoughts on the latest acquisition of X?"

CLIENT: "That is really interesting you asked….."

You ask the set out second question and you get their feedback, thoughts and input. You can use these information to market to them in the future or to create a small report which you can use to market.

Having the second question will increase the time that you are able to spend in the phone and will enhance your chances of building that relationship with the client.

# Telephone Zen

When on the telephone, you need and should be completely Zen-like in the way that you focus. Now, it can be hard to have focus on just the telephone calls when you are in a busy office with all that noise, but there are some simple ways that you can create focus.

The first one is to turn your emails off. Emails are an addictive source of time wasting. They distract you. And to be fair, if you are batching properly, you don't need to be on your emails all the time, especially when you are on the phone.

Secondly, turn all notifications off on all social media and all apps. You do not want them pinging up on your phone. T

Thirdly, when you're on the phone and you want to focus, what you need to do is get everyone in the office into the habit of not asking you questions if you're on the phone.

Now, a great way of doing this is standing up because no one wants to come up to a crazy person who has stood up on the phone talking. They are clearly mad or very busy.

So stand up when you are making your phone calls.

People will not want to disturb you. It could be they're very important and very busy. And alas, it will increase your focus.

And depending on how organized you are and what sorts of CRM system you have, what you can do is print off your call lists for the day, and with those prints of call lists, you can then focus on those calls without even a computer being turned on.

# Ask and go silent

When you are on the phone with a prospect, or face-to-face with a candidate you should always ask questions.

Asking questions is vital in your work as a recruiter.

However, one lesson that is generally not taught to recruiters in the art of shutting up and being quiet or what is sometimes referred to as the golden silence.

Being quiet is important, especially after you have asked a question. When you ask a question you should always then stay silent and the reasons for this is people hate silence, it forms an uncomfortable break that people want to fill.

So when you ask a question to a client and then you go quiet they will fill the void. By filling the void they may give you the response you want, or tell you information they want to keep to themselves.

So ask questions, but remember to be and stay silent after you have asked the question.

# LinkedIn Video

LinkedIn Video is your newest and most exciting avenue to reach your followers and have a real impact on every recruiter's favorite platform.

LinkedIn video is videos created using the LinkedIn app.

The reason you should be using this is very straightforward, it is quick and easy to use. It will get you in front of your audience and LinkedIn favor it in their algorithms.

So get creating videos: Below we have outlined five ideas that you use straight away:

1) Jobs update. Have a job that you are working on? Talk about it for a minute highlighting three positive points.
2) Friday industry news roundup - a rundown of the 5 biggest stories that week.
3) Daily advice video for job hunters - short quick videos to help.

4) Big breaking news in your industry - when the news breaks put your comment and spin on it.
5) Videos with candidates you are representing exclusively.

# Mindful LinkedIn

LinkedIn is great. All those candidates just sitting there waiting to be headhunted.

It is every recruiter's dream. That is partly why it is so successful.

However, when on LinkedIn you need to be mindful of why you are there. To help with this mindfulness you should spend 90 minutes every Friday afternoon on LinkedIn focusing on a few simple but important tasks.

These tasks are outlined below. You should send three prospects an interesting article via LinkedIn that may be helpful for them. Why?

It shows you are thinking about them and adding value and not just asking for ££££. Clear you LinkedIn notifications, say happy birthday and congratulate people on new jobs.

It is nice, gets your name out there and makes you look active too Linked In.

Connect with all the clients and candidates that you spoke with this week and add them into your network.

Comment on five new stories on your feed. Clear out all read messages as well.

Do as much of the above every Friday and it will increase your presence on the site but will also show LinkedIn you are active.

Being active means, you will place higher in the rankings which what we all want.

# LinkedIn welcome

# messages

When you have a new connection on LinkedIn, you should welcome everyone.

You should always say hello. It's courteous. It's polite. It's a nice thing to do.

What you shouldn't do is sell, sell, sell at them.

The worst thing that you get is a message saying

"Hello, I'm a recruitment consultant. Will you buy and spend £10,000 with me, please?"

It's awful. It doesn't necessarily fit the purposes at the time of that person and it makes you look bad.

So what should you do? Essentially, you should do three things. You should say hello. You should thank them for connecting.

You should say, "These are my contact details should you need to get in contact with me off LinkedIn."

And then you should ask a question, like "Is there anything I could help you with today?" And then just leave it at that.

A week later, send them a piece of content they will find useful. That will have a bigger impact on people than a rush to sell, sell, sell.

# Use LinkedIn's desktop

# app

To be fair, I am a massive fan of this application. I downloaded it via the Microsoft Store and I cannot, and I repeat, I cannot say enough about it. It is brilliant.

What you get is a fantastic piece of software that keeps LinkedIn in its own separate programme, meaning that you are not having to necessarily have it open as a tab on your Internet Explorer.

However, you can dip into it quickly and without much effort. It looks lovely and it's worth keeping.

It's good for productivity and Linked In likes you using it as well.

Essentially, it's also good for your own rankings because LinkedIn likes people who like using their apps rather than on the webpages.

So, download it and you will be blown away.

# Create a group on

# LinkedIn

Groups on LinkedIn are forgotten about, but they can be an excellent way of creating a dedicated audience that you can use throughout your recruitment career even when you move on from your current company. Why?

Because you're able to get a bunch of like-minded people together in one place and own that space.

This is a bit of a golden opportunity.

So, what you want to do is you want to create a very specific group to the type of people you are recruiting and then invite all the contacts that you have, and through social media sharing platforms like Hootsuite, send specific updates that they will find useful week in, week out.

And over time, it will build, grow and take on a life of its own. So for example, if you recruit Java developers in Manchester, call it Java Manchester or something like that.

Then just keep inviting them, and over time, it becomes your own little community.

People will share stuff onto the group and it becomes essentially like a little haven where other recruiters can't spam your best contacts.

# Model your keywords

Are you wanting to appear at the top of LinkedIn searches for your niche? Of course, you do. This is one very quick hack that can get you to the top of the LinkedIn search.

Copy your competitor who is top of the tree. When you are doing your research, search what you want to know for - say a Java Recruitment in Manchester. Put Java Recruiter in LinkedIn and see who appears at the top.

Study their profile carefully and then do the following things.

1.  Ensure that your profile is 100% complete.
2.  See how many times they mention the keywords that you find important e.g. Java.
3.  Rewrite your profile keeping in mind that density of keywords, the location of keywords and number of keywords is important to the rankings.
4.  Share content related to this subject matter on a regular basis so candidates in this field visit your profile.

And say to Linked In, this person is Mr. Or Mrs. Java Manchester. In time you will slowly move up the rankings.

As with all things SEO and Search it take time. But this time well spent that will pay back later on.

# LinkedIn Daily

We mentioned the need to stay off social media platforms as they can be a time sink and have the amazing ability to get you angry.

However, with LinkedIn this is very much a different kettle of fish. The reason that this is different with LinkedIn is because how LinkedIn's algorithms work.

When they are ranking people to list at the top of searches they use a formula that includes both keywords, relevancy and activity.

How the exact formula or algorithm works is kept a secret, however, activity is an important part of it.

LinkedIn wants you on the platform, engaging and talking with people so that you will click on adverts, thus generating profits.

Most recruiters are active on LinkedIn, but not active in the appropriate way for the algorithms. So how much activity and what type of activity should you engage in?

We recommend that everyday you share on the platform one status update. Comment on five posts and like ten other posts. This should keep you looking "active" to LinkedIn.

# Adverts that Put

# candidates off

It may seem counterintuitive, but when you write an advert, you actually want to put lots of candidates off applying.

Lets be fair, a lot of people who apply for your jobs are rubbish, are no good, and waste your time.

So what you want to do is you want to repell the time wasters by writing adverts that are very, very specific to the job but also include something that means that they have to put in a bit of work.

So for instance, ask them to put something in the subject heading because if they don't put "that" something in the subject heading, you know they don't pay attention and, alas, are a rubbish candidate and you can get rid of their CV straightaway.

It may seem harsh, but if they cannot follow basic instructions from an advert, they are  not going to follow basic instructions in a job. Thus, are rubbish.

So, follow different ways of repelling candidates.

So, for starters, when you write the advert, write the advert in a way that is very, very appealing to a very specific person that you want to attract. So instead of "Has experience as a credit controller," say "

Has experience as a credit controller for five years within a manufacturing firm in the Greater Manchester Area."

The difference between the two is that you are being far more specific and so credit controllers who maybe have six months' experience will hopefully not apply.

# Ask for advice from

# candidates

Whenever you are headhunting anyone, what you do not want to do is do an aggressive headhunt.

What you want to do is do a soft headhunt by asking for advice. This generally has a better impact than asking people directly because it essentially makes you look good and it allows them the time and space to think about any role or decision you have put in front of them.

So how do you use a soft headhunt by asking for advice? When speaking to a candidate about a role, mention that you would like to pick their brains about a position that they might be interested in, but also that you'd like some advice as well.

Tell them about the role and then you ask for their advice, be flexible in giving them the time to take advice. And what you may find is that if the role is genuinely of interest to them, they will put their hands forward.

What you may find is you have to give the candidate time to think. This is a good thing. Why?

Because you've had time to think, you've had time to allow the ideas to not be so shocking to the candidate, but also, you've not come across as pushy, which is important because looking pushy is always bad because no one likes a pushy recruiter.

Neither do I really, to be quite fair. So, give it a go and see what happens.

# Pain and Pleasure

Understanding a candidate's motivations is important and as a recruiter, it is vital that you take the time to understand what pain is motivating them to move from a job and what pleasure points they are seeking to achieve from this move.

Why do you need to know the pain and pleasure points of each candidate that you are dealing with?

Firstly, understanding what they want and don't want from a job will allow you to ensure you are putting forward a candidate who is suitable and mentally able to put up with the role you are putting them up for.

Secondly, you will be allowing the candidate to be truthful and only serve you better in the long run.

Thirdly, during the process, you will have increased influence on the candidate as you will know what is and is not in their best interests.

# Are they polite?

Politeness is an important feature for any successful candidate.

The reason for this is simply a candidate that has manners and is polite is less likely to screw up the interview.

Now I know what you are thinking, politeness is nonsense. The chances are all candidates will be polite and courteous when they meet with you but are they polite to waiters if you are meeting them in a restaurant or are they polite to your receptionist when they turned up.

Although this can seem slightly less than useful the last thing you want is a candidate who is not polite going into client offices all blasé and treating the receptionist poorly and not getting the job.

# Become a CRM Jedi

Day in, day out, you will be using your CRM and ATS to get work done, to find candidates, to find clients, essentially to do your job.

Now, many people get a cursory bit of training when they start at a company, some on the job tips:

"Here you go. Click here. Click here. Do this," and then are just left to it by their company. And that's probably because most people do not fully understand their CRM software.

What you want to do is become the CRM Jedi in your office. Why? Because this will allow you to find multiple ways of leveraging and enhancing your work processes.

Many CRMs are very powerful pieces of kit, but sadly are not used in the way that the very clever boffins who put them together intended.

So they create the programmes and then 90% of the features are not used.

So, what you should do? Go online of course. Put in the name of your software into YouTube and there will be a whole host of videos that will tell you how to get the absolute most out of your CRM and will probably save you a massive amount of time, effort, and thought daily.

So, give it a go and look it up.

# Micro-Outsourcing

Who says outsourcing is just for FTSE100 or Fortune 500 companies?

We certainly do not think so. Micro Outsourcing is a brilliant way to hack through your to do list and get small, simple tasks done by an expert freeing up more of your time.

Depending on the project it can cost from as little as £5 all the way up and into the hundreds depending on the project you are setting and the skills you are utilizing.

The benefits to using micro-outsourcing are:

Quick - I have had logos designed and finished in 24 hours.

Cheap - I have had whole websites built for £100. Experts - The work is done by experts who know their stuff.

Trusted - Each seller has a ranking and track record that you can see and scrutinize as well as protection that payment is only in stages and not all upfront.

The best sites are People Per Hour, Fivrr and Upwork. When using these sites you will feel a great sense of accomplishment to get the tasks sent off and done in a jiffy.

# Ask for exclusivity

Simple, quick life hack here for any recruiter. When you take on the role, ask, "Can we be the exclusive recruitment consultant on the position?"

Ask every time because if you do not ask, you do not get.

And asking for the role exclusively, although hard, will pay dividends in the end.

If you do not ask, you do not get!

# People buy from you, not companies

It is the hiring manager or the HR manager who buys from you. It is not XYZ Corporation. That person will probably still buy from you if they move to another company.

The reason is they have bought into you.

So, what you want to do is develop numerous contacts at a company because those people move on, and when they move on, the way the company procures recruitment may change.

So, by developing multiple contacts, you increase your chances of sales in that company, but, when Dave moves from XYZ Corp to ABC, he may be on the phone to get you involved with recruitment there.

So, develop multiple contacts. It helps with business development now and potentially in the future.

# Whoever is asking the questions is in control of the conversation.

They are the ones that are dictating where it goes and where it goes to next.

So, you want to always be asking questions because you stay in control and it allows you to guide the conversation to where you want it to be.

Remember, it is your time, it is your call, and it is your responsibility to ask these questions.

So, for example, if a candidate asks you a question about something, let's say, "What is the salary for the role?" what you do is you ask, "What salary are you looking for?" because in that way, instead of them finding out that the role is paying 40 to 50, you may find that they're only looking for 38.

So, you might have a bargain on your hands. But if they hear it's 40 to 50, they then know to ask for at least 40. So that's a good example of why you should stay in control. Ask questions.

Stay in control. And it just makes you more effective in every conversation and in every engagement.

He or she who asks the questions is in control When you are in a conversation with a candidate, with a client, with a gatekeeper, with your boss, with your spouse.

# Wake up and stay up

If you want to get up in the morning early, refreshed, and ready to go, you need a good night's sleep.

However, you will also need a waking up routine. A waking up routine is just as important as a bedtime routine.

Essentially there is a process to waking up and staying up.

Firstly, have your phone across the room, not next to you, or your alarm clock across the room and not next to you.

So, when the alarm goes off you have to physically get out of bed and walk to the phone/alarm. Next, have a glass of water ready to drink next to the alarm clock or phone.

Lastly, once you have drunk the glass of water do five press-ups. This will get you awake and keep you awake.

Going across the room means you have to step out of the bed and walk to the alarm to turn it off. The further you have to walk, the more likely you are to stay up.

Drinking the water hydrates, you and will start to kick start the brain into going from sleep to awake mode.

And doing five press ups will get you active, will get the heart pumping, and will get you thinking that you are awake.

Once you've done this, go downstairs or leave the room. Doing this everyday will keep you awake.

That's just a brilliant way of staying awake.

# Sleep like a caveman

What you want to do is you want to sleep like a caveman.

Why? Because cavemen got sleep.

Why? They did not have TVs, the internet, and they did not have mobile phones or artificial light.

Meaning they had a natural pattern of sleep that coincided with the going down of the sun. We all need and want to replicate this.

The simplest way to do this is to do these three things.

1) Dim the lights to replicate sunset. If possibly get a illumination alarm clock that replicates sunrise and sunset.
2) No screen time at least one hour before bed - that's no mobile phone, no interest, no TV.
3) Have blackout curtains so that the room is completely dark once the lights are out.

The reason is that as humans, we evolved in a state where as dusk approached, the light dropped and our bodies release sleep hormones that prepared us for sleep.

In the modern world we have lost this key trigger, however through taking the steps above you can at least start to fight back and hopefully get a good night's kip

# Bedtime routines will change your relationship with sleep

Remember when you were a kid and you had a bedtime routine?

The same thing every night. Remember how you would fall asleep quickly. As an adult we generally forget that having a bedtime routine is a wonderful way to end the day and set yourself up for sleep.

Why does a routine work? As humans, we are basically still creatures of nature and habit and do respond to stimuli and habit far more than we give credit.

By creating and keeping a routine that you use each night you will be saying to the subconscious parts of the brain it is time for sleep and wide range of chemicals will be released into your system that will kick-start the process of drifting off.

Below is a model bedtime routine that I try to use.

1. Have a set bedtime.
2. One hour before this bedtime put your phone in the kitchen to charge, turn off your ipad and television. Do not have any of these things in your bedroom.
3. Only use your bed for sleep and do not ever power nap during the day.
4. Dim the lights an hour before bed mimicking sunset. Make sure every morning you get sun on your face within 30 minutes of waking up.
5. Do bathroom stuff.
6. Get into bed and read a light novel until you feel sleepy.

This works for me, you have to figure out your own routine, but it needs to reduce stimulation of the electronic kind, must be kept to and mimics our natural circadian rhythms.

If you have any problems with sleep why not visit the Sleep Foundations website. Just Google (other search engines are available) the sleep foundation.

# Defend from the forces of Chaos

*"A schedule defends from whim and chaos. It is the net for catching days"*

Anne Dillard. Anne was an insightful person.

How many times have you rocked up to work and worked very, very hard but seemed to get nothing done.

You were busy, busy, busy but, you were a busy fool. This is where a schedule can step in and make all the difference. Now for every person a schedule can be very different. If you work on an industrial temp's desk you may need to be in the office earlier compared with say a permanent consultant however.

A schedule should have three things. –

Set times each day or week for important tasks. Time set aside for admin and a level of flexibility within each timeslot.

Below we have outlined a what we think is a great schedule.

8am 10am - Non-sales time - Tasks Review the daily plan, respond and clear your inbox, review new candidates, search current openings, candidate registration meetings, 15 minutes purposeful reading, return urgent client calls, clear any admin, go to client visits.

10am to 12midday - SALES TIME - Business Development Calls, Lead chasing calls, Interview feedback.

12midday to 2pm - Non Sales Time - Submit candidate CV's, clear inbox to inbox zero, call candidates with job offers, feedback and updates, organize interviews, HAVE LUNCH AWAY FROM DESK

2pm to 5pm - SALE TIME - Client calls, Business Development Calls, Chase up CV's, follow up on leads, etc. 5pm - 6:30pm - Approach calls to candidates, update calls to candidate, inbox zero and plan tomorrow.

# Focus on 1%

Now, what we're not talking about here is focusing on the gilded wealth of the top 1% of the Bill Gates and the Mark Zuckerbergs of this world.

What we are talking about here is focusing on the 1% within you, and that's the 1% for getting better. If you focus and aim every day to get 1% better at BD calls, by the end of day 70, you'll be twice as good.

The reason we say day 70 is because of the power of compounding.

If you aim to do one more call every day, by the end of day 70, you will have 1% more calls. You will be doing twice as many calls as before.

A great example of this is to, for example, want to increase the amount of candidates that you find. Aim to have 1% more telephone conversations per day with candidates. Make sure you track it, because it it not fact if it is not tracked.

So focus on being 1% better and doing 1% more, and within no time at all, you will double your statistics.

# Kill Procrastination in an instant

Before writing this Life Hack I spent 15 minutes reading up about how the US supreme court works on Wikipedia. Okay, that is a lie, I was looking at funny cat videos on Instagram.

Anyway, I was procrastinating like a champion.

If there was an Olympic medal for procrastination I would probably miss the final because I was scrolling through Doug the Pugs Facebook page.

Anyway, I am even procrastinating in the middle of this life hack.

To kill procrastination in an instant you first need know what your triggers are. For me the triggers are the following, my to-do list, business development calls and doing my accounts.

What triggers your procrastination could be triggered by anything, finding out what they are is half the battle. When I was trying to figure out what my triggers are I kept a log and the pattern became clear very quickly indeed.

Now, once you know your triggers and notice you are procrastinating all you need to do is say this one phrase out loud so other people can hear you "and I am back in the room".

It will snap you out of the funk and get you to focus on the here and now and banish that procrastination. Anyway, back to cat videos on Instagram. Have you seen the one with the cat pushing the glass off the table! I am back in the room!

# Write out every goal

Write out your goals 10 times a day, in hand with a pen and paper. Then read it out loud 10 times. Do this every single day.

Why? Because the subconscious validation of writing out these goals means it gets stuck in your brain and becomes something that to the brain feels real and tangible.

Writing creates a physical and emotional connection in the brain creating a feeling a tangibility in the brain. Reading it out loud all creates the same connection.

Doing both things will daily reinforce your goal and make it believable and achievable to the brain and subconscious.

# Work in 90-day sprints

Have you ever had it that you have been setting yourself an annual goal and it has just not happened?

Before you know it, April has arrived from noware and you have got nowhere near your goal. You joined the gym and you went three times. You were going to learn a language.

You were going to bill £200,000. You may have set yourself 90 days goals, but you did not set yourself up in a working pattern that aims towards these goals?

90 day goals are great but you need to plan your work towards then. Below we set an example. So if you want to bill £25,000 in a 90 day period

Average fee is £5,000. So you need to place 5 people into roles to generate that cash.

Now you need to know your briefing to placement ratio (for our demonstration) is one in five. So to bill £25,000 that means taking on 25 placeable roles to get five placements.

So every week to achieve this £25,000 you need to get 2.1 briefings.

However, given recruitment takes time you may not get all the deals in before the 90 days is up.

So to counteract this you will need to front load business development in the first three or four weeks to get the assignments on an started before the end of the period.

This does not mean you go feast and famine. It does mean you need at the start of the cycle to put in the hours to ensure you 'break the back' of the goal.

# Sell Solutions, not

# Processes

Your recruitment process is not special.

You are not special. However, the solution a candidate provider to the client may be very special indeed.
The candidates that you engage with daily can do some amazing and business changing things for your clients however, the process in which you recruit is not that special?
Why?

There are over 100,000 people employed in recruitment in the UK and innovation on process spreads quickly.

For instance, I started using LinkedIn almost as soon as it was opened to non-invited members now almost every recruiter is on it.

Clients can easily replicate your process - just look at all the former recruitment consultants that are now internal recruiters. However, what they will never be able to replicate is the solutions to their pain points you and the candidates you represent can offer.

Take a brilliant credit controller, they are not a credit controller, but someone who can reduce payment days and free up cash flow this cashflow allows investment and growth. They are not a credit controller but a source of growth.

Representing an excellent Account Manager, they are not an up seller or salesperson. They guarantee the future of the business through retention and gather intelligence on clients' needs for the future.

So, the next time you are speaking with a client (or internal manager) focus on how your candidates can reduce pain points and offer a solution instead.

The candidate is special. The client's problems are special. Your recruitment process is not.

# Hire a VA

Need help with all those dull admin tasks? Need it done by someone which more qualifications than your entire team?

Want it done for a reasonable price?

If you said yes to all three, I bet you said you, and why wouldn't you. VA's are the secret weapon that many entrepreneurs and businesses swear by.

So, what is so great about hiring a virtual assistant from India or the Philippines?

1) Both locations have a great pool of highly educated graduates that are exceptionally keen to work and learn.

2) The wage differential means that you are able to get rudimentary tasks done at a fraction of the price of a domestic staff member doing them.

3) Many providers of VA services will even cover holidays, so you get coverage 5 days a week 52 weeks of the year.

To get you started to check out Tasks Every Day, Timetc and Ask Sunday   India and the Philippines have really led the way in virtual assistants however, over recent years this trend has also progressed to the UK and the US and with a quick Google search you can find many great local assistants.

# Do not neglect hobbies, pastimes and your social life

All work and no play make Jack a dull boy as the saying goes.

Personally, when is started my business I totally forgot that I had friends, a social life, hobbies and pastimes. My rationale at the time, which was flawed, was that to be successful I had to sacrifice everything.

Everything. Looking back this was all rather short-sighted and counter-productive. When after around three years of killing myself I realized I had to improve the diversity of passions and interests in my life and rediscovery old hobbies and rebuild bridges after being a very poor friend.

The change was profound. My stress levels dropped. In my day job, I became more efficient and I also developed happiness and contentment which spilled over into my daily recruiting.

When things went wrong I was more controlled and composed. I had regained perspective. Now, it is very easy given the long hours and rich rewards on offer in recruitment it is easy to become very myopically focused.

Just remember there is more to life than placements.

# Chrome Plugins

Chrome is great. It is by far the best internet browser on the market. It is just lovely. It has all the great Google Search facilities. But one of its most neglected features, especially by recruiters, is the Chrome plugins that you can download via the Google marketplace.

Normally for free. Some of these plugins are an absolute godsend and huge time savers.

What I would suggest is that you get on there, have a look, and go out there and find out what's out there.

These are some of the ones that I use: Zoho Recruitment Zoho CRm Buffer Hunter.io Grammarly

They are great and can be found at

https://gsuite.google.com/marketplace/

They save me time. They save me effort. And with just a click of a button, you can do so many things.

So get in there, start exploring, and you'll find a whole treasure trove of things that are interesting.

Remember Chrome is the best browser with great plugins.

WooHoo!

# Have Lunch

So, did you take a proper lunch break today?

Yesterday?

Anytime in the last week?

The depressing thing is that most people who work in offices in the 21st century just do not take time for lunch. It is a very sad indictment on the way we work and live.

In Britain according to the Telegraph newspaper the average worker takes only a 34-minute lunch break, and for many those 34 minutes are just scrolling through Facebook whilst eating at their desk.

Compare that with the Germans (who are by far more productive per hour than the average British worker) where an hour and a half is not unheard of, many employers still have a canteen where people sit down to eat together. That beats cat videos on Facebook.

Personally, I did the same until the power and miracle of a lunch hour was shown to me.

Once I started working for myself and started taking lunch breaks (thanks to my partner making me) everything changed when it came down to the lunch hour.
So what are the benefits of taking a lunch break away from your desk?

Social interaction with colleagues build bonds that help in the day-to-day team working of the business.

It de-stresses and gives perspective by getting your mind on other things. Allowing your subconscious to do the rest. It is good for health - getting out of the office or going for a walk instead of sitting is good for you and will promote wellbeing.

It invigorates your working as you are fresher for the afternoon.

No carb crash - as you are not chucking in a Boots meal deal into you month as quick as possible before getting back to the phone you will not get the mid-afternoon carb crash as you will have eaten mindfully, slowly and probably less.

So when it is your next lunch break, take it.

# Gray is the new Black

Mobiles are addictive things.

They're brilliant though, I for one, for years, was addicted to Angry Birds. Mobile phones can also be a killer on productivity, steal family and friends time and damage sleep.

They are probably the 21st century cigarettes.

There is one simple, quick and easy way to reduce the addictiveness and the desire to want to be on your phone.

It is called grey-scaling.

What is grey scaling? Essentially, you are turning all the colors black and white. So it's like an old 1950s movie but on your phone. It essentially kills the blue haze background your phone off produces.

The instant you do this, going on Facebook, going on any app is nowhere near as fun or interesting because the colours are what give it vitality and addictiveness to the brain.

The colours help to create that dopamine hit. By going on grayscale, you won't want to be on your phone as much and you will be able to focus during work on the day to day stuff.

# Ask me anything

Thank you for reading all the life hacks. I hope you have found it to be an enlightening and interesting read.

We have on last Life Hack for you. If you have any problems, please do ask me anything.

My email address is
joseph@thenakedrecruiter.com

# A Big Thank You

Thank you for taking the time to read this book. It has been a joy to research, write and study. I had set myself a challenge at the start of 2018 to write a book and I did it by the end of April.

Thank you ever so much again for taking the time to read this book It has been an interesting learning experience.

What gave me inspiration was a saying: "Those who can do. Those who cannot teach." For a long time I thought that this was a swipe at teachers, however, after careful thought, it occurred to me that this was actually about using teaching to become accomplished in the subject matter.

By studying these life hacks I have become a better recruiter and I hope over time, you will also become a better recruiter as well.

The way in which this book is written, there is not much need for a conclusion, however, below

I have outlined how you can keep in touch with me and drop me any questions, thoughts, feelings or suggestions that you have. We also appreciate funny memes jokes and pictures of dogs as well.

# How to Contact Me

I would really love for you to get in-touch and let me know your thoughts on this book. It would be fantastic to hear from you!

You can email me at joseph@thenakedrecruiter.com

You can follow us on twitter @nkdrecruiter

If you love Facebook we have a Facebook page

You can also visit the Naked Recruiter blog at http://thenakedrecruiter.com the website is being constantly updated so please do visit again and again.

# Further Reading

We have created a special recruitment focused reading on The Naked Recruiter that you can view.

Hope onto Google, type "site:thenakedrecruiter.com – reading list" and you will find the reading list.

Printed in Great Britain
by Amazon